Rising Up, Falling Down

by Craig Hammersmith

Content and Reading Adviser: Joan Stewart
Educational Consultant/Literacy Specialist
New York Public Schools

Spyglass BOOKS

COMPASS POINT BOOKS

Minneapolis, Minnesota

Compass Point Books
3722 West 50th Street, #115
Minneapolis, MN 55410

Visit Compass Point Books on the Internet at *www.compasspointbooks.com*
or e-mail your request to *custserv@compasspointbooks.com*

Photographs ©:
Comstock, cover; PhotoDisc, 4; Two Coyote Studios/Mary Walker Foley, 5; PhotoDisc, 6; Visuals
Unlimited/Bruce Clendenning, 9; Two Coyote Studios/Mary Walker Foley, 11; PhotoDisc, 12; Two Coyote
Studios/Mary Walker Foley, 13; Visuals Unlimited/Jim Whitmer, 15; Two Coyote Studios/Mary Walker
Foley, 17; PhotoDisc, 18, 19; Two Coyote Studios/Mary Walker Foley, 20, 21.

Project Manager: Rebecca Weber McEwen
Editor: Jennifer Waters
Photo Researcher: Jennifer Waters
Photo Selectors: Rebecca Weber McEwen and Jennifer Waters
Designer: Mary Walker Foley

Library of Congress Cataloging-in-Publication Data

Hammersmith, Craig.
  Rising up, falling down / by Craig Hammersmith.
      p. cm. -- (Spyglass books)
Includes bibliographical references (p.   ).
Summary: Explains the cycle of evaporation, condensation, and
precipitation that provides fresh water to the earth.
  ISBN 0-7565-0233-0 (hardcover)
  1. Hydrologic cycle--Juvenile literature. [1. Hydrologic cycle. 2.
Water.] I. Title. II. Series.
  GB848 .H36 2002
  551.57--dc21

                                    2001007339

Contents

Water World

Water covers most of planet Earth. Most salt water is found in the oceans. *Fresh water* is found in lakes, streams, rivers, and ponds.

Did You Know?
All living things need water to survive.

Water is found
in a lake and in
the clouds floating
in the sky.

Recycled Water

All of the water that's on Earth right now is all that we'll ever have.

Earth

Nature has been *recycling* water since the beginning of time, using the water cycle.

Did You Know?
The word *cycle* means "circle" or "wheel" in Greek.

The Water Cycle

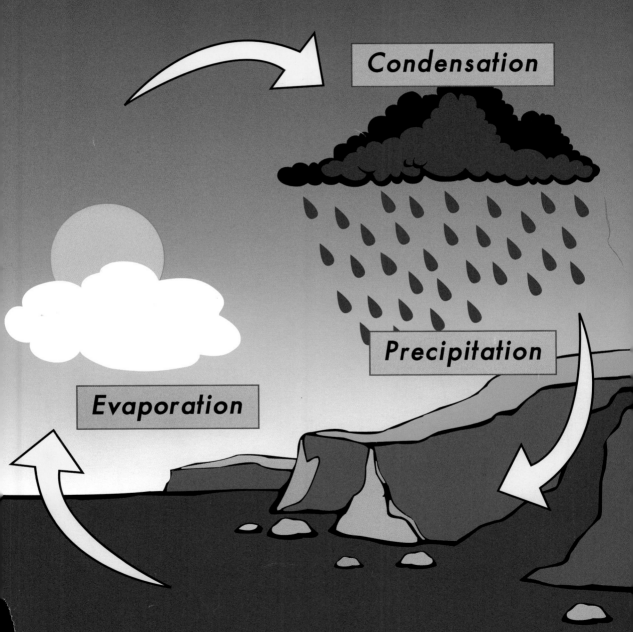

Going Up!

Evaporation is the first step in the water cycle. Evaporation happens when the sun heats water enough to change it to a gas. This gas, which is called vapor, then rises into the air.

Did You Know?

When there is a lot of water in the air, your sweat can't dry and you feel hotter.

Water vapor in the air

Vapor Turns to Water

When water vapor floats up high, the air gets colder. When the air is cold enough, the water vapor cools and turns back into water droplets. This is called condensation.

Did You Know?

You can see condensation when you take a shower! Hot water vapor in the air condenses when it touches the cooler mirror.

Condensation
on a mirror

Making Clouds

It takes many water droplets or ice crystals to make a cloud.

Did You Know?

Clouds that form high in the sky are made of ice crystals. They can look thin and wispy.

Cirrus clouds

Cumulus clouds
are full of water.

Coming Down!

All clouds are made of water. When the water in the clouds gets too heavy, the water begins to fall toward Earth. This is called precipitation.

Did You Know?

All clouds are made of fresh water. This is because when salt water evaporates, the salt stays behind in the ocean water.

Girls in rain

Rain, Sleet, Hail, Snow

Rain is water that falls when the air is warmer. Snow falls when the air is cold enough to freeze water. *Sleet* and *hail* form when the water droplets fall through both cold and warm air.

Did You Know?

When wind blows a big water droplet high into a cold cloud, the droplet freezes and becomes a hailstone.

Snow

Sleet

Water Returns to Earth

Once the water has fallen back to Earth, the water cycle can begin again!

Did You Know?

People can harm the water cycle. *Pollution* from cars can mix with  water vapor. Then the rain is full of pollution, too.

Rainbows happen
when sunlight shines
through the water in
the air during or after
a rainstorm.

Make a Terrarium

A terrarium is a small, covered container where you can see a water cycle.

You will need:
- a jar with a lid
- potting soil
- small gravel
- small plants
- water

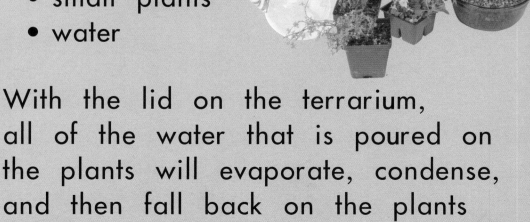

With the lid on the terrarium, all of the water that is poured on the plants will evaporate, condense, and then fall back on the plants over and over again!

1. Put in five
   handfuls of gravel.

2. Add six handfuls
   of potting soil.

3. Put in two or
   three plants.

4. Water the plants.
   Put on the lid.

Glossary

condensation—when a gas cools and becomes a liquid, such as water

evaporation—when a liquid, such as water, heats until it becomes a gas and then rises into the air

fresh water—water that has no salt

hail—frozen lumps of ice that fall from a cloud

pollution—human-made dirt that harms air, water, and all things that live in it

precipitation—water falling to Earth as rain, sleet, snow, or hail

recycling—using over and over again

sleet—freezing rain

Learn More

Books

Branley, Franklyn M. *Down Comes the Rain*. New York: Harper Collins, 1997.

Fowler, Allan. *The Earth Is Mostly Ocean*. Chicago: Childrens Press, 1995.

Frost, Helen. *The Water Cycle*. Mankato, Minn.: Pebble Books, 2000.

Web Sites

Brain Pop
www.brainpop.com/science/seeall.weml
(click on "water cycle")

Many Adventures of Drippy the Raindrop
www.kimballmedia.com/Drippy

National Geographic
www.nationalgeographic.com/world/amfacts/
clouds_q1.html

Index

GR: I
Word Count: 205

From Craig Hammersmith

I like to camp in the mountains near my Colorado home. I always bring a good book and a flashlight so I can read in the tent!